Linking art to the world around us

artyfacts
Our Bodies

Contents

WRITTEN BY Rosie McCormick

Strong bones

Just like a building, your body needs a frame to hold it together. The body's frame is called the skeleton. It is made up of over two hundred bones. Your skeleton gives your body its shape. Your skull, for example, gives your head its round shape. The bones in your limbs make them long and thin, and curved ribs shape your chest.

PROTECTION

Some bones protect organs in the body. The skull protects the brain. The ribs protect the heart and lungs.

MOVING FRAME

Your skeleton works with your muscles to allow you to move about. Muscles are connected to your bones by stetchy bands called ligaments. These pull at the bones to make them move.

SPONGY BONES

Bones are solid on the outside, but spongy in the middle. A strong covering protects the hard bone, and in the centre is the spongy marrow. Thousands of cells are always busy rebuilding the bone to keep it strong. They also help the bone to heal if it is broken.

BIG AND SMALL

The longest and strongest bone in your skeleton is the femur, which is in your thigh. The smallest bone is the stirrup bone inside your ear.

Skeleton man

Make a funny skeleton man with shiny bones to hang on your wall

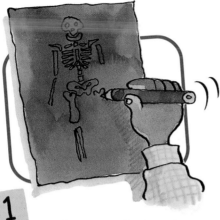

1 With a pencil, sketch the skeleton bones onto white paper. This is your plan.

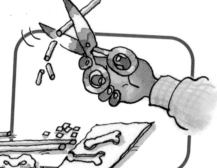

2 Using the plan as a guide, cut out skeleton bones from the white card, straws and polystyrene pieces.

3

Stick the pieces onto a piece of black card to make a skeleton man.

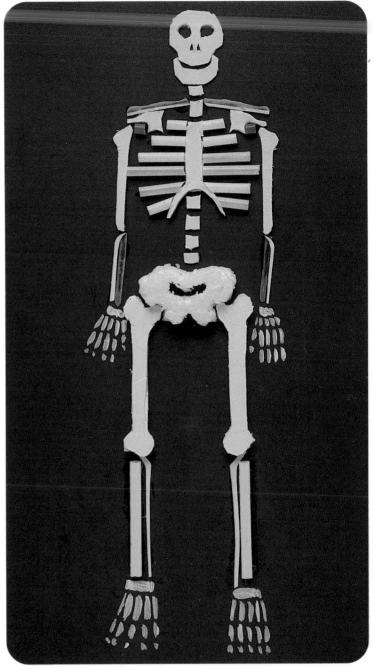

Add extra details to your skeleton with a white pencil.

5

Art at our fingertips

If you press the tip of your finger onto an ink pad and then press it onto a piece of white paper, you will be able to see the fingerprint you leave there. No one else in the world has fingerprints exactly like yours. Your footprints are different from everyone else's too.

FINGERPRINTING

A long time ago, slaves or prisoners were sometimes marked by tattoos so that they could always be identified. Much later, photographs and body measurements were used. But the practice of fingerprinting was not developed until the 1880s when scientists were able to show that it would be almost impossible for two people to have the same fingerprint. It wasn't long before fingerprinting was introduced as a way of identifying criminals. Since then it has become an important tool in criminal investigations all over the world.

Everyone has a special fingerprint. Can you see the difference between these four patterns?

This magnified photo of a fingertip shows the arch pattern.

LOOPS AND ARCHES

If you look at your fingertips you will see many tiny lines, or ridges. These lines make patterns of loops and circles. Each finger has a different design. Scientists classify fingerprints into four groups. They do this by studying the pattern made by the ridges. In the 'loop' group the ridges curve back over on themselves. In the 'whorl' group the ridges make a circular pattern. The ridges in the 'arch' group arch upwards as they cross the finger tip. The fourth group is known as 'accidental' because this pattern has no fixed form. Today, we use computers to classify and compare fingerprints.

6

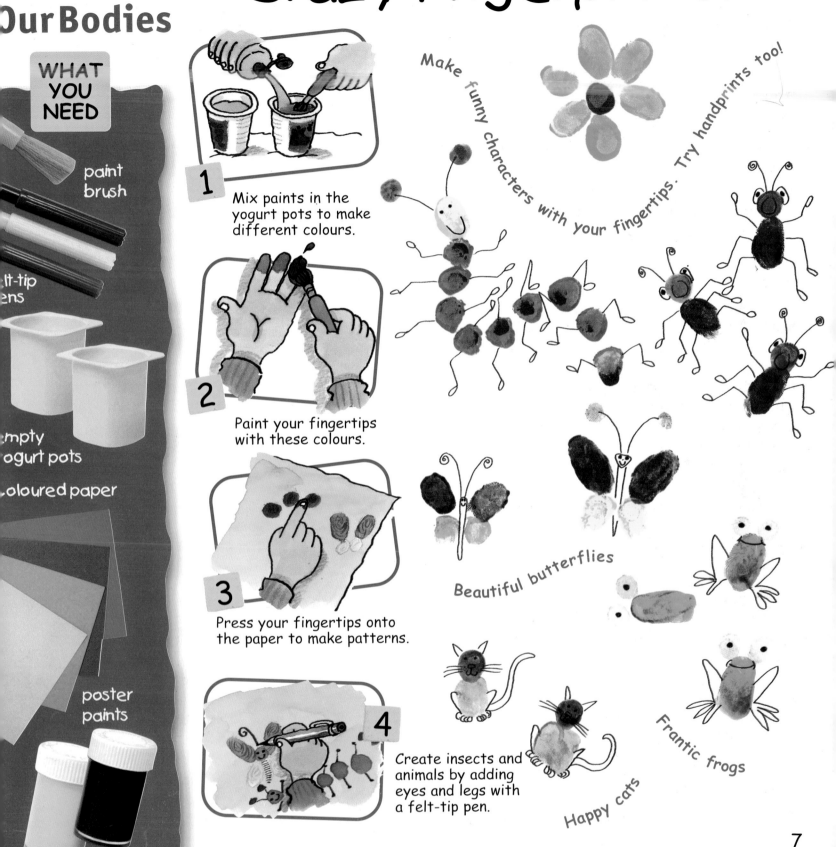

Crazy fingerprints!

Our Bodies

WHAT YOU NEED

paint brush

felt-tip pens

empty yogurt pots

coloured paper

poster paints

1 Mix paints in the yogurt pots to make different colours.

2 Paint your fingertips with these colours.

3 Press your fingertips onto the paper to make patterns.

4 Create insects and animals by adding eyes and legs with a felt-tip pen.

Make funny characters with your fingertips. Try handprints too!

Beautiful butterflies

Frantic frogs

Happy cats

7

Joints and levers

atch an athlete sprint along a race track and then leap over a hurdle. Follow the moves of a dancer, curling and bending in an energetic performance. Think about an acrobat or gymnast making moves with their bodies that seem almost impossible – jumping, cartwheeling or doing flips in the air. All of them are using body movement to the full.

BENDY SKELETON

The human body is made up of many different bones which are linked together in a framework, called a skeleton. The places where the bones fit together are called the joints. Most joints, such as those in our legs and arms, allow the bones to move.

DIFFERENT KINDS OF JOINTS

Some joints, such as our elbows, knees and knuckles, work like a door hinge or lever. They are called hinge joints. Other joints, such as our wrists, ankles and backbones, or vertebrae, are called ball and socket joints. In this type of joint, the end of one bone can turn in the hole at the end of the other. Ball and socket joints allow parts of our body to twist or swivel. These different joints let our skeleton bend and stretch in different ways.

MUSCLE PAIRS

The bones that meet at each joint are moved by muscles. Muscles move bones by pulling themselves in. They can only stretch out again when another muscle pulls them back. This is why many muscles work in pairs.

Lively acrobats

Connect up the joints to make a bendy body mover

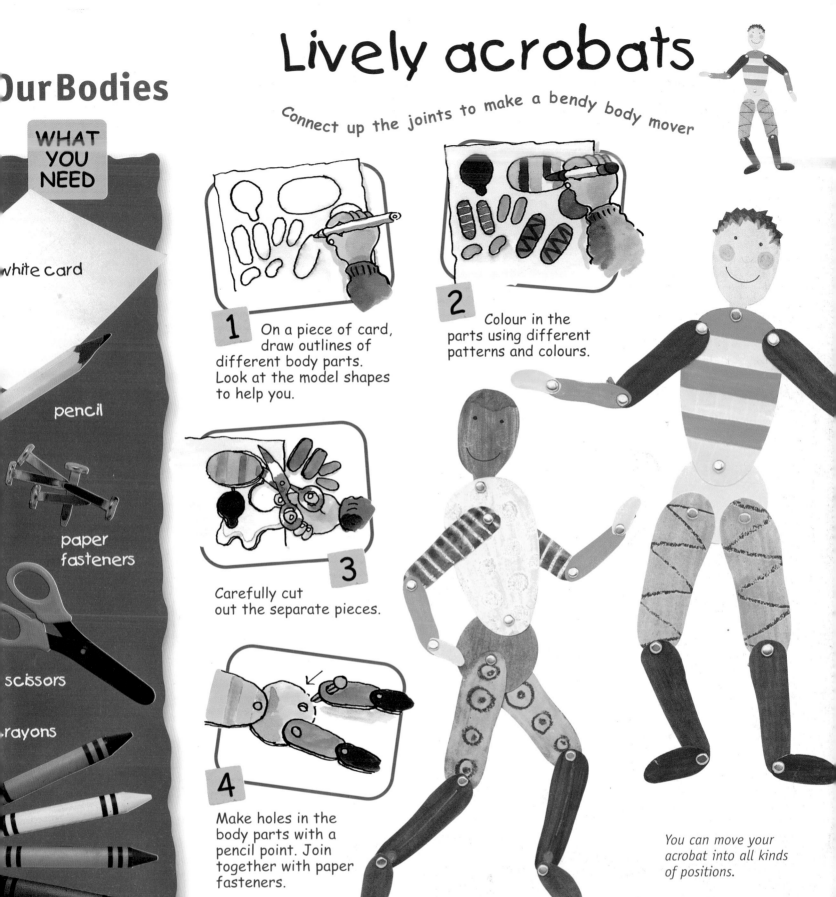

WHAT YOU NEED

white card

pencil

paper fasteners

scissors

crayons

1 On a piece of card, draw outlines of different body parts. Look at the model shapes to help you.

2 Colour in the parts using different patterns and colours.

3 Carefully cut out the separate pieces.

4 Make holes in the body parts with a pencil point. Join together with paper fasteners.

You can move your acrobat into all kinds of positions.

9

Eye-opener

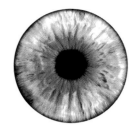

LIKE A CAMERA

Your eyes are very important sense organs. They work a bit like a camera. When you look at an object, the light that reflects, or bounces off it, travels into your eyes. The light enters your eyes through the pupil. This is the black dot in the centre of the coloured iris. Then the light passes through the clear lens behind. The lens focuses the light, and an upside-down image forms on the retina at the back of the eye. The retina is connected to the brain by the big optic nerve. The optic nerve carries information signals about the image to the brain. The brain interprets the image and turns it the right way up.

LIGHT AND DARK

Did you know that your eyes behave differently in different light? In bright light the pupils close up small, but in dark light they open wide. You also have two kinds of light-detecting cells in your retina. Rods see only in greyish tones, but work well in dull light. Cones see colour and take over in bright light. Each eye has about 120 million rods and 6 or 7 million cones.

Did you know that about 70 per cent of the information you store in your brain is in picture form? Your eyes collect information about the world around you as thousands of different kinds of images. These include the words you read, as well as the things you look at. Most of what you know comes from seeing.

EYE WASH

Every time you blink, your eyelids wash tears across your eyes. This cleans and protects them. When you cry, some tears flow away through two tiny tear ducts in the corners of your eyes, and into the back of your nose. This is why you sometimes get a runny nose when you cry.

Wacky shades

card

scissors

pencil

glue

ter

coloured
acetate

tissue
paper

Make your own designer collection of eye wear

1 Draw two wacky-shaped lenses on card. Add arms, fold them back and and cut out.

2 Screw up bits of different coloured tissue paper into little balls, and glue them onto one pair of shades.

3 On the other pair of shades, paint on glue and then tip on coloured glitter. Shake off the loose bits.

4 Finally, glue down pieces of acetate onto the back of both pairs of shades.

1

Black, white and yellow

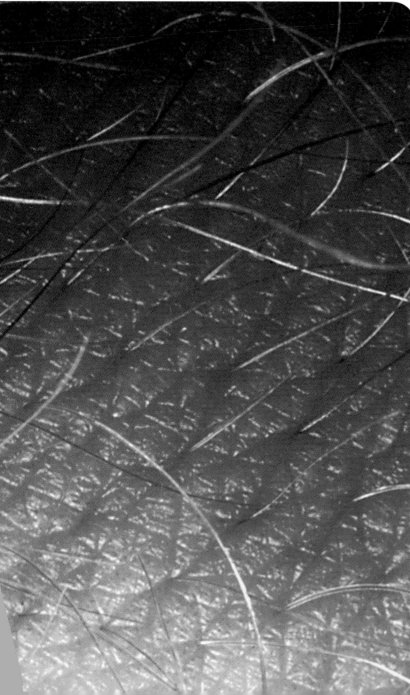

Our skin is the largest body organ we have. It covers us completely and protects our inside parts. The colour of our skin depends upon how much melanin it produces. Melanin is a brown pigment or colouring which is formed by cells called melanocytes in the outer layer of our skin.

MELANIN IN THE FAMILY

All people have about the same number of melanocytes in their skin. But the melanocytes of dark-skinned people make more melanin than those of light-skinned people. You inherit your skin colour from your parents.

MORE MELANIN FROM SUNLIGHT

Melanin protects you against harmful rays from the sun. When you are outside, the skin that is exposed to the sunlight creates more melanin. This makes it a browner colour. In some people, the melanin builds up to form spots, or freckles. More freckles appear on people's faces and hands because these are the parts which are exposed to the sun most often.

PROTECTION

People from very sunny climates tend to have a lot of protective melanin in their skin. In very cold countries, such as Sweden, people tend to have pale skin that produces much less melanin.

A close-up photograph of skin.

Multicultural collage

Create a fascinating frieze of different-coloured faces

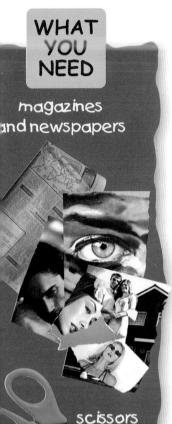
Look in magazines and newspapers for pictures of people from different countries.

3 Cut out the faces, arrange them so they slightly overlap each other, and glue them to the board.

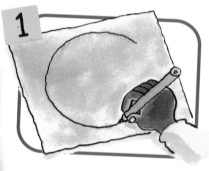

1 Draw a shape on your backing board and cut it out.

2

13

Keeping fit

In our modern, high-tech world it's easy to spend lots of time in front of a TV or a computer. But to stay healthy, your body needs exercise. Getting involved in sport is a fun way of keeping fit. It also allows you to be with friends and to play your part in a team.

STAYING HEALTHY

If you exercise regularly, you will feel happier, healthier – and keep your body in shape too. You will also have more energy, so you can work and study to the very best of your ability.

ABOUT MUSCLES

Exercise helps to build and tone your muscles, making them firm and strong. This doesn't mean that you have to have big muscles, just efficient ones. Exercise also stretches your joints, making them stronger and more supple.

GOOD EXERCISES

Walking, running and jumping make your heart stronger, improve your circulation and help you to breathe properly. You can rollerblade, skip, swim, play football or ride your bike. Most of these sports develop balance, hand and eye control and your ability to think and plan quickly.

Fitness freaks

Make figures doing press-ups, handstands and keep-fit exercises

WHAT YOU NEED

plaster of Paris

paints

wire

strips of fabric

paintbrush

bucket bowl

newspaper

1 Cover the work surface with lots of newspaper.

2 Cut lengths of wire. Twist and bend them to form a rough but strong outline of an exercising figure.

3 Mix the plaster of Paris in the bucket or bowl, following the instructions on the packet. Then stir in the strips of fabric.

4 Wrap the strips of fabric, one by one, around the figure so that the wire is totally covered.

5 Leave to dry, then paint your figure.

You could make a group of prancing dancers

Coils and curls

Look closely at your arms. Can you see the tiny hairs growing out of the skin? They protect your skin and help to keep you warm. Hair grows all over your body, but most thickly on your head – you have about 100,000 hairs growing from there!

DEAD OR ALIVE?

Hair is made from keratin, the same material your nails are made of. It grows from tiny pits, called hair follicles, in your skin. Each hair is rooted inside its own follicle. Only the base of the hair, where it is growing, is alive. The strand above the skin surface is dead. That's why cutting your hair doesn't hurt.

HAIR ALL OVER

There are fine hairs all over your body. The only hairless parts are the palms of your hands, the under parts of your fingers, and the soles of your feet.

When boys and girls become teenagers, they start to grow more body hair. Boys grow coarser body hair, especially on the face.

STYLE IT RIGHT!

Your hair can be cut, shaped, decorated, twisted and twirled! How a person's hair looks is an important part of their appearance. For hundreds of years, people have enjoyed creating all kinds of different hairstyles.

INHERITED HAIR

The kind of hair you have depends on the shape of your hair follicles. Oval follicles make wavy hair. Round follicles make straight hair, and flat follicles make curly hair. In different parts of the world, people have different kinds of hair. In parts of Africa, many people have dark, curly hair. In Scandinavia, many people have very straight, fair hair. You usually inherit the kind of hair you have from your parents.

Hairy head models

Create your own salon of hairstyles!

1 Soften the clay by rolling it in your hands.

2 Make a head shape.

3 Cut equal lengths of wool and tie them together in the middle with more wool, to make a woolly wig.

4 Repeat using strips of silver paper.

Stick small twigs onto a length of plasticine to make a mohican hair cut!

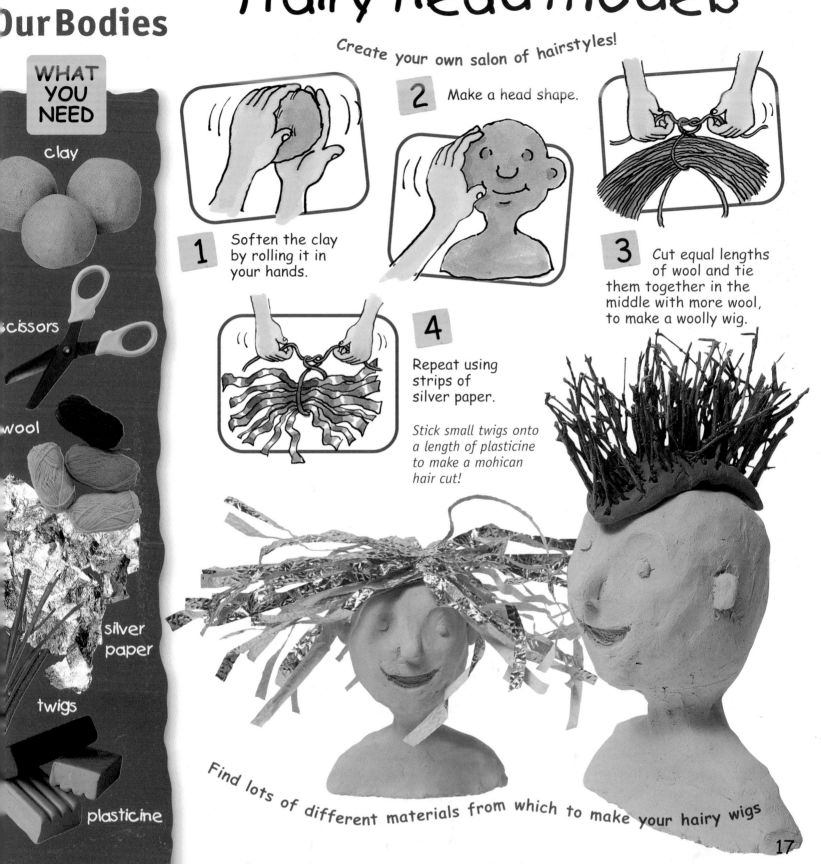

Find lots of different materials from which to make your hairy wigs

17

Sharp edges

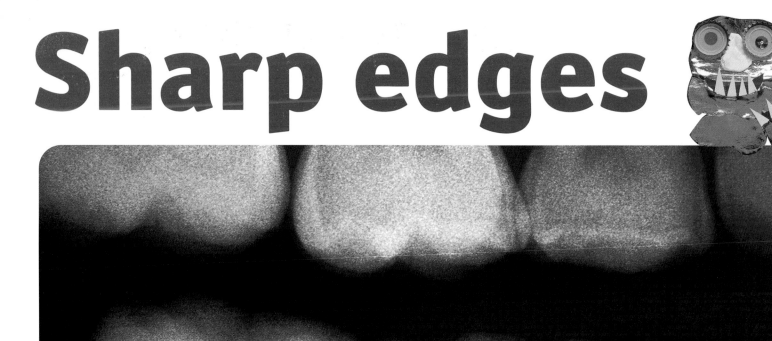

When you are born, your teeth are usually hidden inside your gums. They begin to push through when you are around six months old. At about three, you have 20 baby teeth – which begin to fall out when you are about six! But, by the time you are grown-up, 32 strong adult teeth have replaced them.

STRONG STUFF

Your teeth are covered by enamel, the hardest material in the body. Strong roots anchor them into your jawbone. This is because they must last many years of grinding, chewing and chomping!

CUT, CRUSH AND CHEW

Look in your mouth to see your three different kinds of teeth. The sharp, flat incisors at the front cut and slice. The pointed canines next to them grip and tear. And the wide, flat molars at the back crush and chew. Your teeth all work together to make sure your food is properly broken up into little pieces before you swallow.

KEEP BRUSHING

Brush your teeth at least twice a day! If you do, they will stay healthy and strong. If you don't, tiny bits of food will collect in your mouth and harm your teeth and gums. And remember! Check-ups at the dentist will keep your teeth in good shape.

Monster gallery

WHAT YOU NEED

material

paints and brush

black felt pen

coloured card

thick white card

tissue paper

pencil

glue

glitter

scissors

1 Draw the outline of a monster face and hands on a piece of coloured card.

2 Cut out the face and hands and the open mouth part. Stick onto your mounting card.

3 Create sharp teeth by cutting triangular shapes from thick white card. Stick them into the mouth of your monster.

4 Make sharp nails and horns from the thick card and stick these onto your picture.

5 Use a thick piece of tissue paper to make a padded nose.

6 Cut shapes from the tissue paper and thick card and stick down for the eyes. Use a black pen to outline the eyes.

Make a family of toothy monsters!

Use other materials – glitter, sequins, foil, buttons – to create different monster faces and claws.

Taste buds

Do you realise how amazing your tongue is? As well as helping you talk, it guards your body from harm. It tells you whether the food or drink you are about to swallow will be good or bad for you. If something tastes nasty, sharp, bitter or sour, your tongue will warn you not to swallow it!

WORKING TOGETHER

Together your nose and tongue detect, or sense, the different chemicals in food and drink. Tiny smell sensors in the roof of your nose, and taste buds on the surface of your tongue, send messages along your nerves to the brain. Your brain interprets the messages and lets you know whether the flavours are delicious or disgusting!

SWEET OR SOUR?

About 10,000 tiny taste buds are scattered across the surface of your tongue. Those at the back react to bitter flavours, and are the most sensitive. Those on the sides recognise sour and salty tastes, while the taste buds on the tip pick up sweetness. Find out how important your nose is for tasting, with this flavour challenge: put on a blindfold, hold your nose, and taste something salty, something sweet and something sour. Which flavour is which?

MOBILE MUSCLE

Your tongue is a very mobile muscle. You can wiggle, stretch, twist and turn it! As well as tasting, it helps to squash and move food around in your mouth. It also removes pieces that get stuck, and pushes chewed food to the back of your throat for swallowing. Your tongue also helps you to shape the sounds of speech. Try this: hold the tip of your tongue and say something. Now what was that you said?!

Taste buds magnified many times

Salt dough fruit basket

WHAT YOU NEED

- flour - 3 cups
- oil - 1 teaspoon
- water - 1 cup
- salt - 1 cup
- paints and brush
- baking tray
- bowl and spoon
- rolling pin
- varnish
- plastic bag

1 Put the oil, water, salt and flour in a bowl and mix with a spoon to form the dough.

2 Knead the dough and place it in a plastic bag for one hour.

3 Roll out the dough. Make a basket, and fill it with lots of different fruit shapes. Place them on a baking tray.

4 Bake in the oven for about 1 hour at gas mark 2 or electric 150°C.

5 Leave to dry for a day and then paint. Add a coat of varnish to stop the baked dough from flaking.

Bake and decorate a selection of tasty glazed dough foods

21

Micro invaders

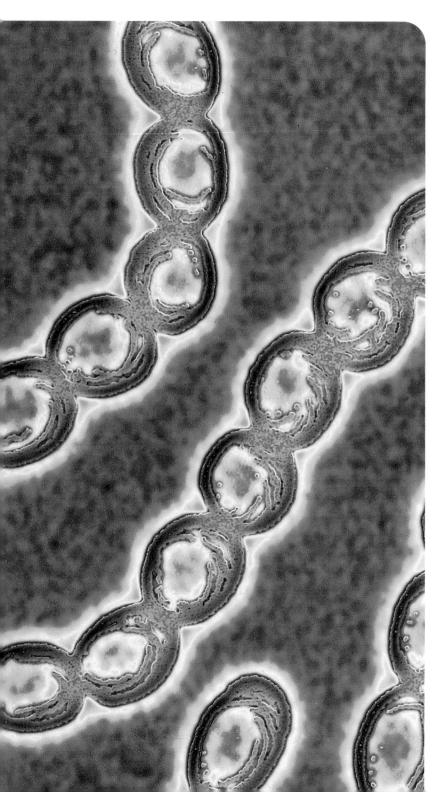

Germs are so small that you need a microscope to see them. Most of the time, you don't even know they are around. They float about in the air, on water, and they are even found in food. But when germs get inside your body, they can make you ill.

GOOD AND BAD

Bacteria are tiny, one-celled bodies, or organisms. They stay alive by feeding on their surroundings – and that could be inside you! Bacteria can be good or bad for you. Some keep your digestive system healthy and fight off other germs. But others can give you infections and make you feel ill.

IT'S CATCHING!

A virus is a germ that travels from person to person in drops of water sprayed out of your mouth and nose when you cough or sneeze. If a virus gets into your bloodstream, it can quickly make you ill. Chickenpox and mumps are two fast-spreading illnesses caused by viruses. You usually only catch them once. When you get ill, your body makes special defence cells, called antibodies. These attack the virus and will recognise and destroy it if it returns.

FIGHTING BACK

Antibiotic medicines fight bacterial infections, and injections called immunisations fight dangerous viruses. You can stop bad germs from getting inside your body by washing your hands often, especially before eating.

Sequin chains

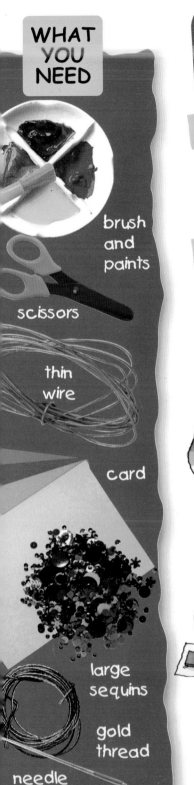

brush and paints

scissors

thin wire

card

large sequins

gold thread

needle

1 Make holes in the ends of each sequin with a needle.

2 Cut a piece of wire, thread and loop it through the sequins, attaching them to each other as shown in the picture.

3 Cut a strip of card and paint it.

4 Thread the lines of sequins onto the card.

Try making a dangling chain curtain with beads and buttons

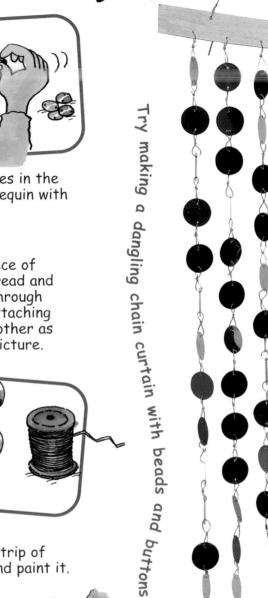

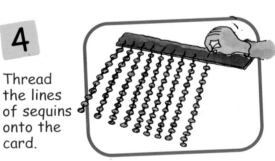

Make holes in both ends of the strip of card. Insert a length of gold thread through each hole and knot it. Hang from a window and watch the sun reflect patterns around the room.

Pulling faces

If you look at the faces of people in a crowd, it is easy to spot the differences between them. Different people have different facial features. Each person's eyes, nose, cheekbones or mouth look slightly different. Facial features are hereditary, which means they can be traced back through the family. They may also be related to where a person lives.

BLUE EYES, BROWN EYES

Why do some people have blue eyes and some brown? It depends on where they live and where their ancestors lived. Brown eyes give better protection against the sun's rays, so people who live in sunny climates tend to have brown eyes.

SMILES AND FROWNS

Smiles and frowns, as well as all other movements of the face, are made possible by the facial muscles. These small muscles pull in many different directions.

NOSES

Noses can be big or small, wide or thin, hooked or straight. Your nose warms, cleans and moistens the air you breathe before it reaches the lungs. Nerve endings at the back of your nose detect smells. Some people have wider nostrils than others. This may have developed from the need to take more air into the lungs in very hot countries.

Funny faces gallery

You can also create a funny faces gallery using family photographs

Make sure you ask permission before cutting up a photograph that does not belong to you.

WHAT YOU NEED

- pencil
- glue
- magazine pictures
- scissors
- coloured card
- white paper

1 Cut out different eyes, noses, mouths and ears from magazine pictures.

2 Stick these down on paper to create funny faces.

3 Draw a face shape around each 'funny face' and cut it out.

4 Mount your gallery of faces on a large sheet of coloured card.

25

Beating hearts

SUPER MUSCLE

Your heart is a kind of hollow muscle about the size of your fist. Its job is to pump blood around your body. It works by squeezing and then relaxing, in rhythmic beats. Each beat of your heart pushes blood through a system of tubes called veins and arteries. In this way the blood carries oxygen and food to all the cells in your body.

PUMPING BLOOD

Your heart is made up of two pumps, side by side. The pump on the left side receives fresh oxygen-rich blood from the lungs and pumps it around your body. This blood gives its oxygen to the body and carries away the carbon dioxide that your cells cannot use. It then returns to the pump on the right side. From here, used blood is sent to the lungs where the waste carbon dioxide is removed and more oxygen is collected. Now the blood is fresh again, ready to be pumped around your body once more.

HEART BEAT

You can hear the beat of a baby's heart when it is still inside its mother's womb. It begins to beat about seven months before a baby is born. You can feel how fast your heart is beating, by pressing your fingers on the inside of your wrist. This is called taking your pulse. Your heart beats faster or slower depending on what you are doing. When you are asleep, your heart beats slowly. When you are running around, it beats faster to increase the oxygen supply to your body.

Some muscles in your body work all by themselves without you realising it. These muscles are called 'involuntary' muscles. Your heart is one of these and works all of your life, without stopping.

Felt cushion

Make a soft cushion decorated with hearts

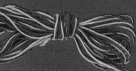

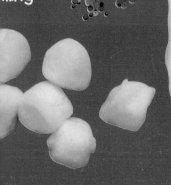

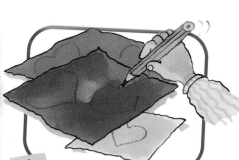

1 With a pencil, draw 4 large hearts (2 on one colour and two on another) and 1 small heart (on a third colour) on the felt. Cut them out.

2 With coloured thread, blanket-stitch the heart shapes onto a square piece of felt.

3 Sew on sequins for decoration.

4 Blanket-stitch 3 sides of the felt square to a second felt square.

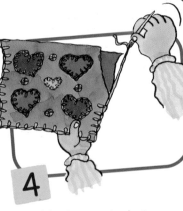

5 Stuff the inside of the cushion with your filling, then close the last side with blanket-stitch.

27

Touch and feel

The hands of a blind person move over a sheet written in braille

How do you know when something is too hot or too cold? By feeling it of course! Even if you couldn't see or hear, your sense of touch would help you to understand the world around you. Try this: put on a blindfold and ask a friend to give you three different objects. You will probably recognise the objects, just by touching them.

LAYERS OF SKIN

You feel things through your skin. Your sense of touch comes from the layer of skin called the dermis. This is filled with minute sense receivers, called receptors. Each receptor is connected by

nerves to your brain. When the receptors detect – or feel – things such as heat, roughness or pain, a message is sent through the nerves to your brain.

EXTRA-SENSITIVE

The receptors are spread unevenly through the dermis. You have more receptors in some areas than in others. For example, the skin on your lips detects heat more strongly than the skin on your elbows. Your fingertips are among the most sensitive skin surfaces you have.

TOUCH AND READ

Blind people can 'read' with their fingertips, using braille. This is a series of raised dots punched in paper. The blind person runs their fingertips across the different patterns of dots. Each pattern stands for a different letter or number.

Textured touch art

WHAT YOU NEED

tissue paper

sponge

rrugated ard

lystyrene

glue

foil

tton ol

sand

hay

string

ncil

ard

scissors

1 Roughly sketch a patterned outline on your card.

2 Experiment with creating textures from the variety of materials you have collected eg: scrunching up pieces of tissue paper; tearing up paper; rolling up string.

3 Glue the different textured items into the patterned sections on your card, leaving one section free.

4 Put glue on this section and sprinkle sand onto it to create a rough texture.

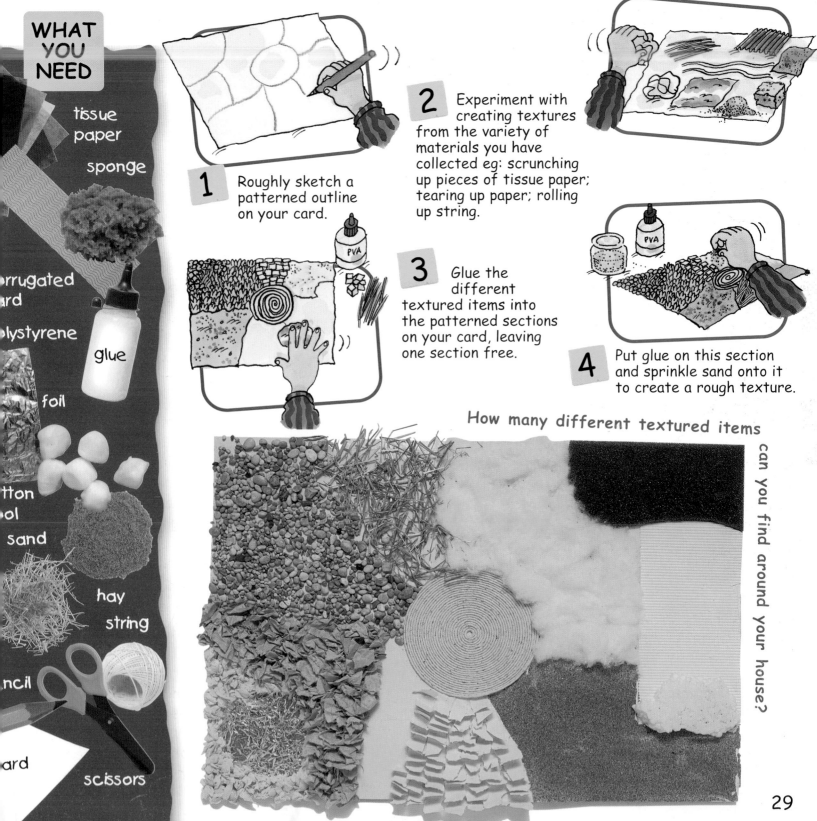

How many different textured items can you find around your house?

29

Throwing and catching

HAND-EYE CO-ORDINATION

When you throw or catch something, the brain acts as a co-ordinator between your eyes and your hands. Being able to catch or throw well depends upon this hand-eye co-ordination.

BRAIN WORK

In order for you to catch a ball, your brain has to work like a computer. When your eye sees the ball coming it sends messages to your brain. From these signals, the brain works out where the ball is and how fast it is moving. It uses this information to move your arms and hands into position, and then to control your fingers so they hold the ball.

Whenever we pick up a ball, it is hard to resist throwing it up and catching it. It seems such a natural thing to do! Many ball games, such as baseball, cricket, rugby, basketball and rounders, involve throwing and catching. It looks easy enough, but it takes lots of brain work to co-ordinate the eyes that see the ball with the hands that catch it.

MAKING A THROW

When you throw a ball, your eyes send signals to the brain, which works out how far away the catcher is, and then how much throwing power your arm must use. It also calculates how fast you should throw the ball, and in which direction it must travel. Signals are then sent to the arm and hands, so they move in just the right way to hurl the ball through the air towards the catcher.

Papier-mâché balls

Make and decorate a colourful set of balls for catching or throwing games

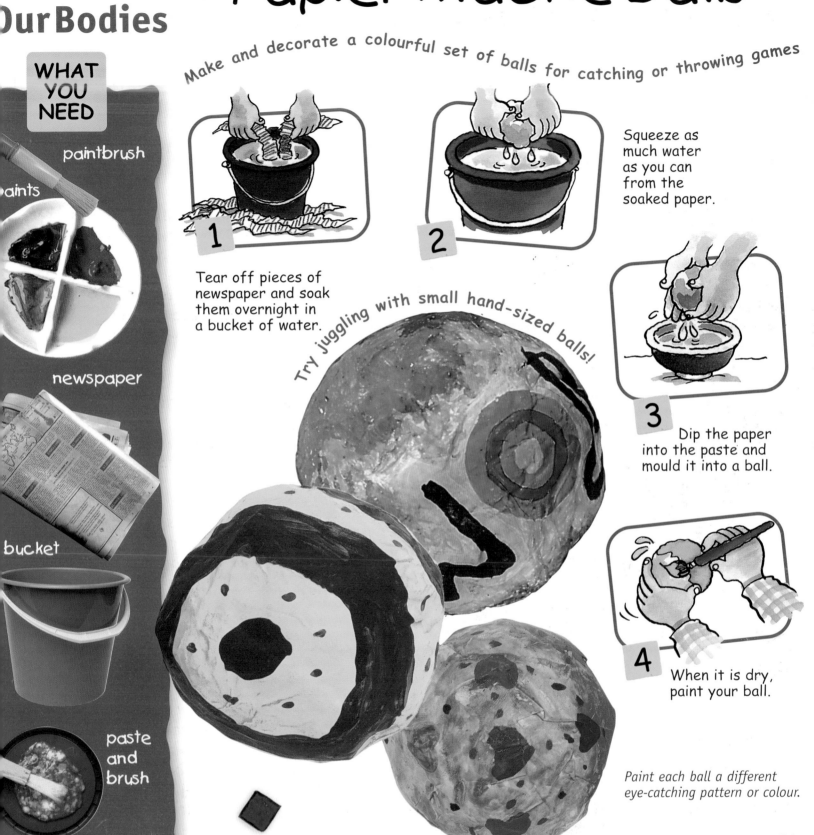

paintbrush

paints

newspaper

bucket

paste
and
brush

1 Tear off pieces of newspaper and soak them overnight in a bucket of water.

2 Squeeze as much water as you can from the soaked paper.

Try juggling with small hand-sized balls!

3 Dip the paper into the paste and mould it into a ball.

4 When it is dry, paint your ball.

Paint each ball a different eye-catching pattern or colour.

31

Brainbox

from your skin receptors, from organs such as your heart or lungs, and from sense organs such as your eyes, ears and nose. Nerve signals travel from the different parts of your body along a network of nerves called the nervous system. When your brain has decoded the information it receives, it sends messages back through the nervous system, telling your body what to do.

A scan of the brain showing areas of activity during speech.

You are the owner of an amazing personal computer — your brain! By making a series of connections, it controls every part of you. It tells you how to smile, cry, think, and blink. It can solve problems, tell you how to move your arms and legs, and let you know whether you are hot or cold. It will help you remember the facts on this page.

SENDING AND RECEIVING

Your brain never stops working. It receives information about the world around you, all the time. The information comes as nerve signals sent

BRAIN PARTS

Your brain looks something like a large, crinkly walnut! It is protected from harm by your hard, bony skull. Your brain is divided into three main parts. Each part has a particular job to do. The largest and most important is called the cerebrum. This controls ideas, feelings and memories. The smaller cerebellum is the part that looks after balance and movement. The part called the brain stem connects with the spinal cord. This holds the network of nerves that carries messages around your body.

LEFT OR RIGHT?

Are you right-handed or left-handed? Your cerebrum is divided into two sides – left and right. One side usually has more control than the other. For left-handed people this is right side, while for right-handed people it is the left.

Circuit board collage

pencil

card

gold and
silver paint

paints
and
brush

tissue
paper

glue

textured
paper

1 Draw a rough outline of your circuit board on a square piece of card.

2 Stick strips of different textured papers and twisted tissue paper around the outline to create circuit lines.

3 Use brightly coloured paint along the lines, and metallic gold and silver paint around the boxed areas on the board.

Jazz up your circuit board with buttons, paper clips and foil

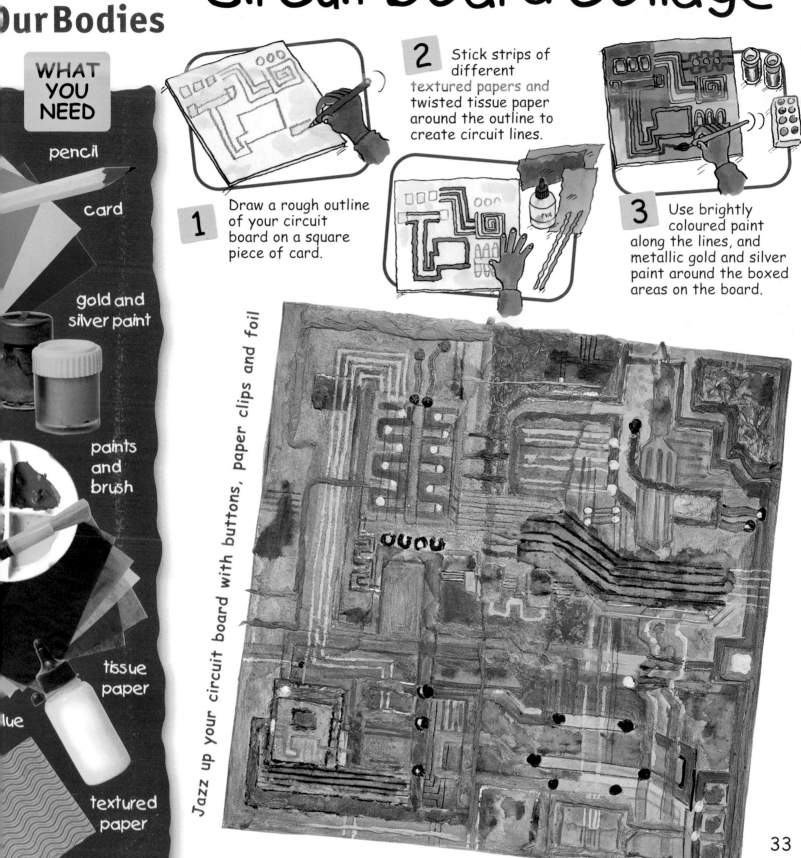

33

Pipes and tubes

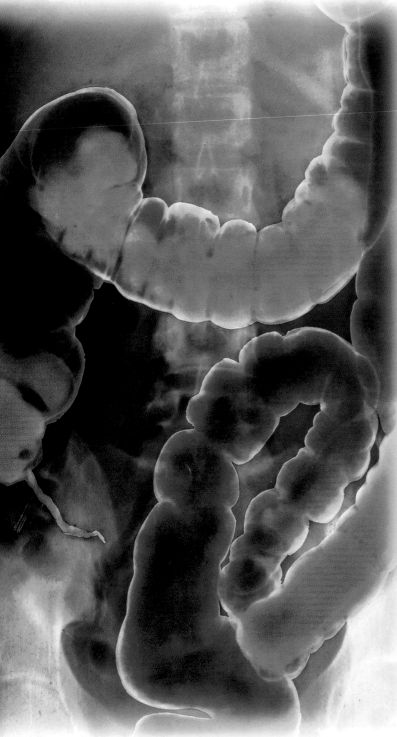

Did you know that after you have chewed and swallowed your food, it goes on a long journey to different parts of your body? On the way it is digested, or broken down, into tiny nutrients that keep you healthy.

Softening saliva

Before you swallow it, food is mixed with watery saliva. This flows out of tubes inside your mouth, called salivary ducts. Saliva softens the food, and begins to break it down to make it easier to swallow and digest.

Squeeze and churn

After swallowing, the food moves down your gullet into your stomach. Inside, it mixes with gastric juices, containing chemicals called enzymes. These break down the food even more so that it can be taken in by your body. Your stomach muscles squeeze and churn the food for up to six hours, until it is a soupy mixture. It is then squeezed through a long, winding tube called the small intestine, where tiny bits are taken into the blood and carried around your body.

Waste disposal

The food parts that your body cannot use are then pushed through another long, coiled-up tube called the large intestine. Solid waste, called faeces, is stored in a part called the colon. Waste water, called urine, is sent from the kidneys to your bladder. When you go to the toilet, the waste squeezes out of your body.

An x-ray of the large intestine.

Shimmering straw art

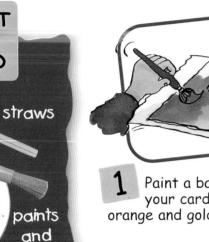

straws

paints
and
brush

glue

thin
card

scissors

glitter

sequins

gold
paint

pipe
cleaners

1 Paint a background on your card using red, orange and gold paints.

2 Cut the straws into different lengths and decorate them with glitter and twisted pipe cleaners.

Create pipe art with decorated card tubes

3 Glue the straws to the card in a variety of patterns.

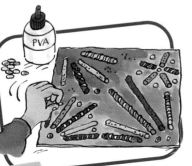

4 Fill the gaps with sparkling sequins.

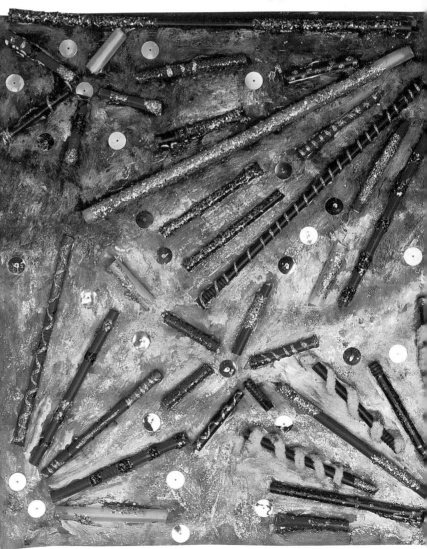

35

Breathing machine

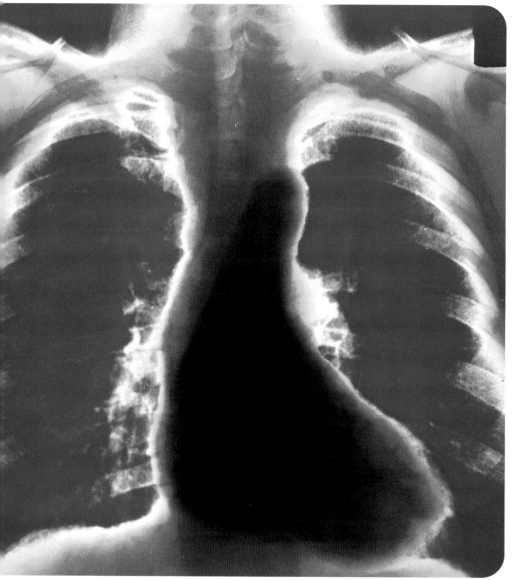

WORKING LUNGS

Your lungs are two large, sponge-like bags, or sacs. Each lung contains millions of tiny spaces, or air chambers. Your lungs fill with air when you breathe in, and empty when you breathe out. They are protected by your bony rib cage, which moves in and out as your lungs take in oxygen and breathe out carbon dioxide. Each lung can hold as much air as a medium size balloon.

IMPORTANT GAS

Every part of your body needs oxygen. Your heart, blood and lungs work together to make sure that this important gas is carried around your body. Because your body cannot store oxygen, it needs a constant supply. Each time you breathe in, air containing oxygen enters your nose, goes down your windpipe and into your lungs. In your lungs, blood vessels absorb, or 'soak up' the oxygen. Then your heart pumps the oxygen-filled blood around your body.

CLEVER BREATH

How do you talk and make other sounds? Air from your lungs is pushed through the opening in your voice box, or larynx. This is like a box with two pieces of skin stretched over it – the vocal cords. When air pushes through, the vocal cords vibrate to make sounds. To feel this happening, put your fingers on your throat at the bottom of your neck and say "Ahhh!".

Every time you breathe you are taking in the oxygen your body needs to stay alive, and getting rid of the carbon dioxide it cannot use. You have two organs inside your chest specially designed for this. They are your lungs.

Puffing bellows

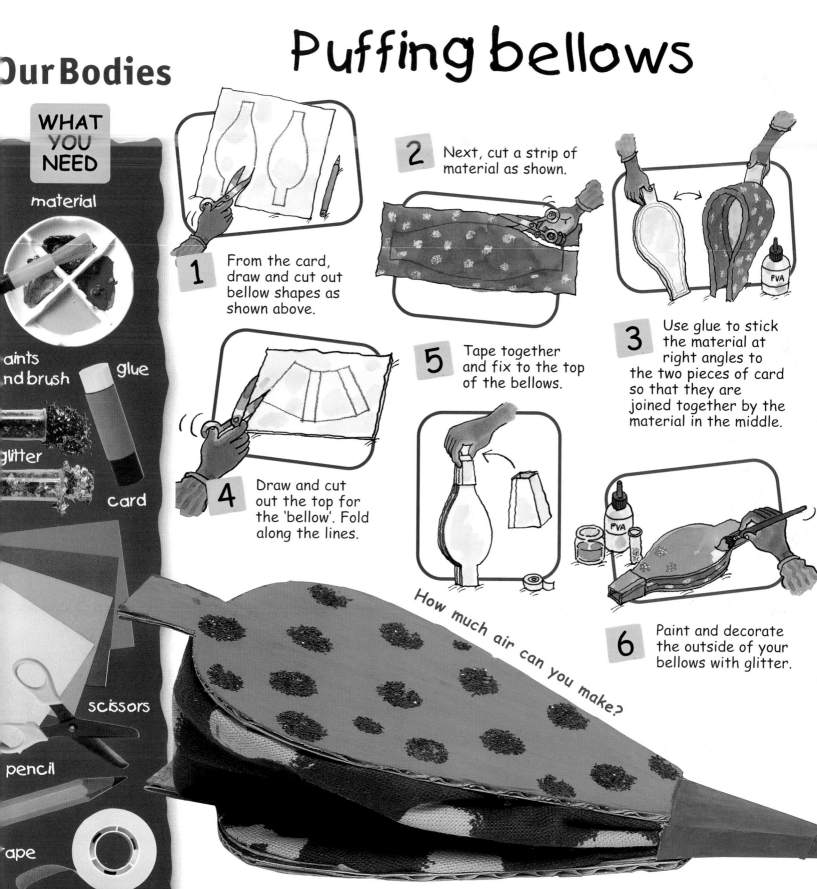

material

paints and brush

glue

glitter

card

scissors

pencil

tape

1 From the card, draw and cut out bellow shapes as shown above.

2 Next, cut a strip of material as shown.

3 Use glue to stick the material at right angles to the two pieces of card so that they are joined together by the material in the middle.

4 Draw and cut out the top for the 'bellow'. Fold along the lines.

5 Tape together and fix to the top of the bellows.

6 Paint and decorate the outside of your bellows with glitter.

How much air can you make?

PVA

Blood-red

Blood is amazing stuff. Did you know that you have about four litres flowing around inside you? It is speeding around your body through a transport system of tubes. The blood is delivering nutrients to feed you, and oxygen and heat to keep your body alive.

Red and white blood cells, seen through a microscope.

TRANSPORT SYSTEM

Your blood travels around your body in small tubes called blood vessels. Thick, muscular blood vessels, called arteries, carry blood that is filled with oxygen. Softer, stretchy blood vessels called veins carry the blood without oxygen. Your heart is the engine that powers the whole system. The right side of the heart pumps blood to your lungs to collect fresh oxygen. Then the left side pumps the oxygen-filled blood all around your body.

BLUE BLOOD

Look at the veins on the inside of your wrist. They are a bluish colour aren't they? That's because your blood changes to a dark-bluish colour as it releases oxygen into your body. But when your blood collects oxygen from your lungs, it turns bright red.

WHAT IS BLOOD?

Blood is a mixture of tiny cells floating in a fluid called plasma. One drop of blood has about 2,000,000 red blood cells, about 5,000 white blood cells and about 2,500 cell parts called platelets. The tiny red cells carry the oxygen around your body. The bigger white cells attack enemy bacteria in your blood, and also make antibodies to fight diseases. And if you cut yourself, the platelets collect together to clot, or thicken, the blood to stop the bleeding.

Splatter painting

Experiment with string and straws to create more splatter art

WHAT YOU NEED

paints and brush

old toothbrush

glitter

newspaper

coloured paper

glue

mounting card

1 Place newspaper down before you start. Put your paper on top of the newspaper.

2 Water your paint down, dab the paintbrush into it and flick your wrist to splatter colours onto the paper.

3 Use the dry toothbrush to create a fine spray.

4 Make circles on the paper with the glue and sprinkle glitter onto them.

5 Mount your splatter paintings on the mounting card.

The inside picture

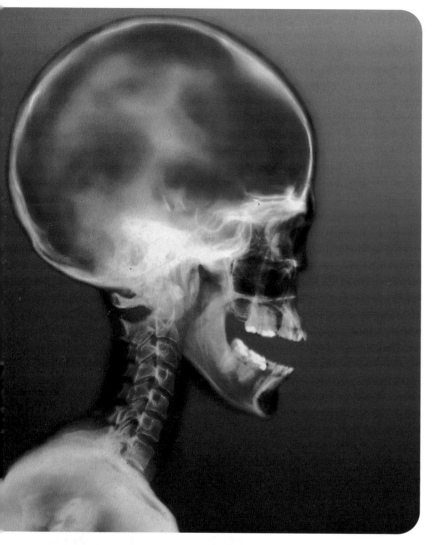

INVISIBLE WAVES

An X-ray is a stream of waves of electromagnetic radiation. These invisible energy waves are like the light waves that come from the Sun, only shorter in length. Unlike sunlight, X-rays can travel through materials such as flesh and skin. This means we can use them to see inside the human body.

X-RAY PHOTOGRAPHS

Radiography is the use of X-rays to photograph the insides of things. It is used in medicine to locate problems like bone damage or tooth decay. It can even be used to build up a three-dimensional image of the body that shows organs, blood vessels and any diseased parts.

CHECKING UP ON BONES

If doctors want to check how children's bones are growing, they sometimes take X-rays of their wrists. If your wrist bones look right on the X-ray, it is likely that all the other bones in your body are also growing the way they should.

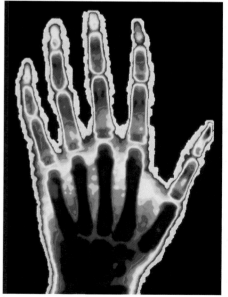

'HIGH TECH' USES

X-rays are often used to look for faults in materials, to study crystals, or to find objects in outer space.

If your skeleton suddenly disappeared, you'd fall down in a heap! Your skeleton, which is made up of all the linked bones that lie under your skin, provides a strong frame for the whole body. The bones are joined together by joints, which allow the skeleton to move. We can photograph the skeleton using X-rays which travel right through the skin.

An X-ray shows all your bones.

X-ray art

You can create an extraordinary X-ray gallery of bony body pictures

1 Using a white wax crayon, draw the outline of a skeleton on tracing paper. Use the picture on the right as a guide if you wish.

Mix a little black paint and water together. Wash over the skeleton with watery paint to reveal your X-ray picture. **2**

3

Try creating skeleton pictures of different animals.

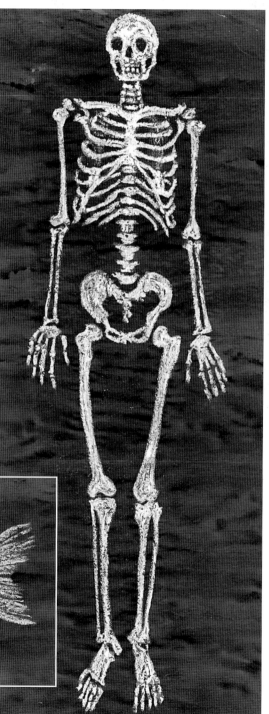

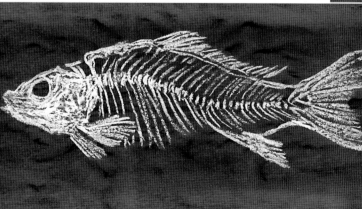

A see-through fish picture

Sound catchers

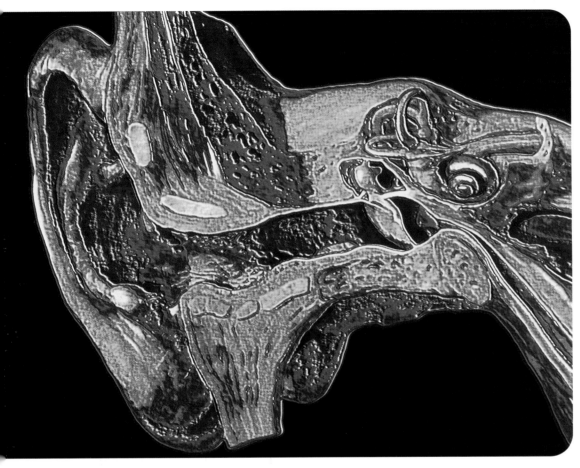

The middle ear contains the eardrum and three tiny bones called ossicles. The inner ear, deep inside, contains the cochlea. This is a bony coil filled with fluid.

SOUND WAVES

When sound waves enter your ear, they make the eardrum vibrate and the ossicles shake. This causes the fluid inside the cochlea to move about. These movements are detected by the cochlear nerve, which sends signals to tell the brain what you are hearing. Your ears react to different kinds of sounds. Test this by listening closely to the noises around you. If a sound is very loud or irritating, how do your ears feel?

A computerised picture showing the structure of the ear.

Like your eyes, your ears collect information about the world around you. Not only can they hear loud noises, such as crashing thunder, they can also hear soft sounds, such as a tinkling wind chime. Your ears are specially designed to 'catch' sound as it moves through the air.

WHAT'S INSIDE?

The ear has three main parts. The ear flap and the ear canal form the outer part. This outer part is funnel-shaped, so sound waves can enter easily.

BALANCING ACT

Your ears do more than help you hear. They also help you to balance. This is because when you jump, skip or run, the fluid inside three small, hollow loops in your inner ear starts to swish and swirl. And as the fluid moves, it touches tiny nerve cells at the bottom of each loop. The nerve cells send messages to your brain. Then your brain sends messages to your body to stop you from falling over!

Tinkling shell mobile

Add shining beads and buttons to make your mobile shimmer and jangle

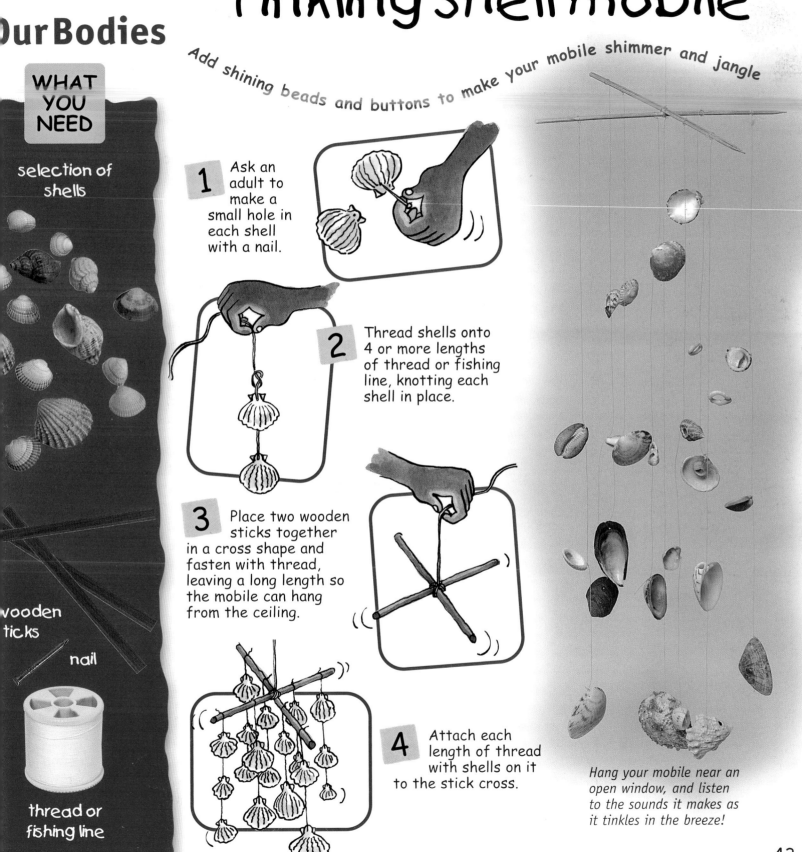

selection of shells

wooden sticks

nail

thread or fishing line

1 Ask an adult to make a small hole in each shell with a nail.

2 Thread shells onto 4 or more lengths of thread or fishing line, knotting each shell in place.

3 Place two wooden sticks together in a cross shape and fasten with thread, leaving a long length so the mobile can hang from the ceiling.

4 Attach each length of thread with shells on it to the stick cross.

Hang your mobile near an open window, and listen to the sounds it makes as it tinkles in the breeze!

43

Body blueprint

In the days before computers, architects and engineers used written plans or drawings of the work they had to do. These plans were known as blueprints. You also have a special set of instructions about how each cell in your body should behave. This human blueprint is found in the centre, or nucleus, of your body's cells. Until recently only your fingerprints could identify you. Now we know that the structure of your special blueprint, or DNA, can give further proof of your identity.

CONTROL CENTRES

DNA stands for 'Deoxyribonucleic Acid', a substance containing the code that decides how every person is built. The DNA molecule in each of our body's cells controls how each cell develops and operates. It also passes its information onto new cells. In this way, DNA provides a master plan for the whole body.

DNA FINGERPRINTING

The pattern, or sequence, of DNA in a sample of hair or body fluid, like saliva or blood, can identify a person. DNA samples are sometimes used by police to help solve serious crimes.

TOO SMALL TO SEE

A DNA molecule is so small that it can only be seen through a powerful microscope. DNA has a complicated structure that, when magnified, looks like two spirals joined together to form a twisted rope ladder. This shape is called the 'double helix'.

This is a model showing the rope ladder structure of DNA.

Twisted choker

You can also make a twisted bracelet and a pair of earrings!

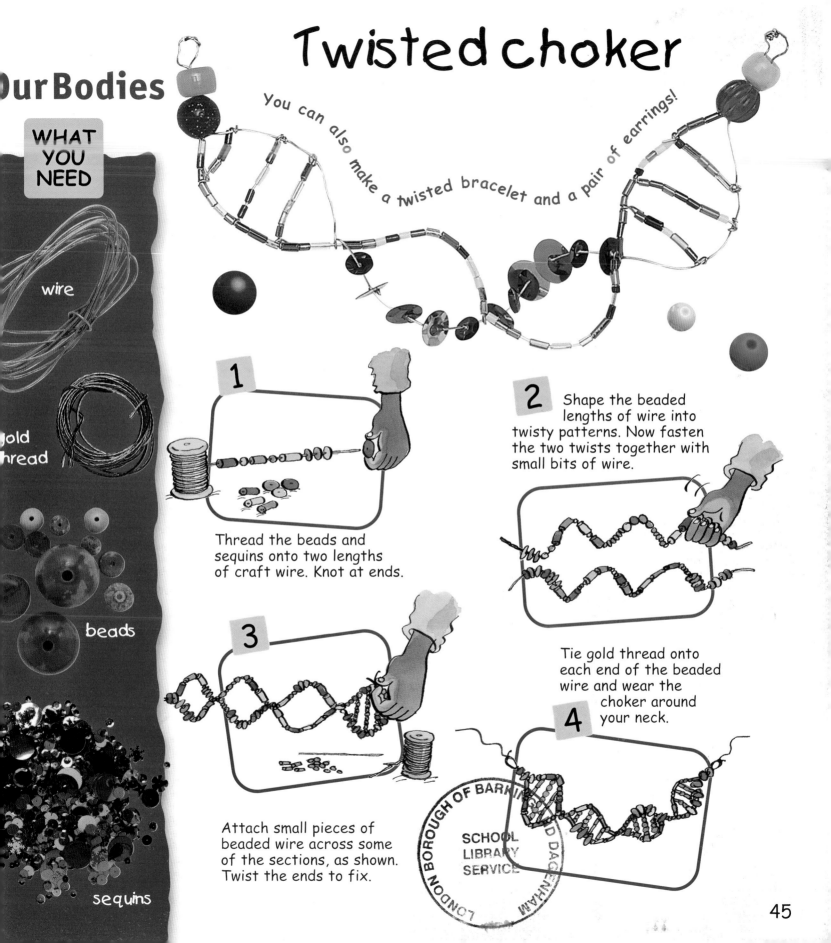

wire

gold thread

beads

sequins

1

Thread the beads and sequins onto two lengths of craft wire. Knot at ends.

2 Shape the beaded lengths of wire into twisty patterns. Now fasten the two twists together with small bits of wire.

3

Attach small pieces of beaded wire across some of the sections, as shown. Twist the ends to fix.

Tie gold thread onto each end of the beaded wire and wear the choker around your neck.

4

45

Glossary and Index

ankle 8

antibodies Defence cells made in your blood that recognise and attack the germs that cause illness. 22

arm 8, 16, 32

arteries The blood vessels that carry oxygen-rich blood around your body. 26, 38

baby teeth The 20 teeth we grow first. They start to fall out at about six years old and are replaced by adult teeth. 18

bacteria Some kinds of bacteria live inside our body and help keep us healthy. Other kinds can cause disease and infection if they get inside us. 22, 38

backbone (or spine) 8, 12

bladder The stretchy bag inside you, made of thin muscle, which fills up with urine. You empty it when you go to the toilet. 34

blindness 28

blueprint A plan that has every single piece of information needed to make something. 44

blood The red, sticky liquid which flows around your body through a network of blood vessels. 22, 26, 36, 38, 44

blood vessels The thin, stretchy tubes that hold your blood. There are two main kinds: arteries and veins. 36, 38

bones 4, 40

braille A system of raised dots representing letters which can be used to spell out words for blind people to feel and read. 28

brain The organ that is the body's control centre. It is made of millions of tiny cells that let you think, feel, remember and control your body's movements. 4, 10, 30, 32, 42

breathing 14, 36

canines The four sharp, pointed teeth you use for cutting. 18

carbon dioxide One of the gases in the air we breathe, but which the body cannot use. 26, 36

cells The living parts of you, which are so tiny you can only see them with a microscope. 4, 38, 44

chest 4

circulation The movement of blood and gases around your body. 14

DNA The shortened name for 'deoxyribonucleic acid', the material found in the cells of everything alive. DNA decides exactly how we are built. 44

digestion Breaking down food into tiny nutrients. 34

digestive system All the parts of your body that the food you swallow travels through, such as the stomach or large intestine. 22

ears 42

eardrum The tightly stretched cover over the middle ear. It shakes when it is hit by sound waves, moving the tiny bones inside the inner ear. 42

enamel The hard material covering the outside of your teeth. 18

eyes 10, 14, 24, 42

facial features The parts of your face, such as your eyes, nose, mouth, cheeks and chin. 24

faeces The solid waste material that collects in your colon. 34

family 24

fingerprint 6

follicles Tiny holes in your skin from which the hairs on your body and head grow. 16

footprint 6

germ A tiny living thing small enough to live inside your body, or to enter your bloodstream from the outside. 22

hair 16

hands 14, 30

head 4

heart The important organ in your chest that pumps blood around your body. 4, 14, 26, 32, 36, 38

46

heartbeat The movement your heart makes as it pumps blood around your body. 26

hereditary The word that describes a body feature you inherit, or get, from your parents or grandparents, such as blue eyes, or curly hair. 24

incisors The flat front teeth that cut and slice your food. 18

infection An illness caused by germs getting inside your body. 22

iris The coloured part of your eyes. 10

jaw 18

joints 8, 14, 40

keratin A tough substance made of protein that is found in the outer layer of your skin and which makes it waterproof. 16

kidneys Two organs inside your body which are part of your digestive system. The kidneys separate the waste urine from useful liquid. 34

leg 8, 32

lens A soft, see-through part of the back of the eye which receives light. 10

ligaments Strong bands of tissue which hold the ends of bones and joints together. 4

limbs 4

lungs A pair of organs which help you breathe. Air is breathed through the nose and sent to the lungs. 26, 32, 36, 38

medicine 22, 40

molars The large, flat-based teeth that grind food. 18

mouth 22, 24

microscope 22, 44

muscles 4, 8, 14, 20, 24, 26, 34

nerve 42

nerve signals Messages that travel along the nerves of the body to the brain. 32

nervous system The system of nerves all over the body. 32

nose 10, 20, 24, 36

nutrients A part of the food we eat that will help us grow and stay healthy. 34, 38

organ Any complete part of the body. The liver and heart are both organs. 4, 32, 36, 40

ossicles Three tiny bones – the stirrip, hammer and anvil - in the middle part of the ear that vibrate when sound reaches them. 42

oxygen A colourless, odourless gas in the atmosphere on which humans depend to breathe. 26, 36, 38

pupil The round black centre in our eyes. 10

red blood cells The cells that carry oxygen in the blood. 26

retina The layer of cells that lines the back of the eyeball. 10

ribs 4

rib cage The framework of ribs attached to the breastbone. The rib cage protects the lungs. 36

sense organs The parts of the body that help you see, hear, touch, taste and smell. 10, 20, 32

skeleton 4, 8, 40

skin 16, 28

skull The hollow bony box that protects the brain. 32

stomach The part of the body where food is broken down. 34

tear ducts The openings to the gland behind the eye which allow tears to flow to the eye. 10

teeth 18, 40

throat 20

tongue 20

urine The waste fluid that your body gets rid of. 34

veins The tubes in your body that carry blood back to the heart. 26, 38

virus A tiny germ. 22

white blood cells The cells in your blood that help fight infection. 38

windpipe The pipe down which air passes from the mouth and nose to the lungs. 36

womb The part of a female body where a baby is formed. 26

x-ray A photograph of the inside of the body. 40